E

Anoɪ

C000007976

methuen | drama

LONDON · NEW YORK · OXFORD · NEW DELHI · SYDNEY

METHUEN DRAMA
Bloomsbury Publishing Plc
50 Bedford Square, London, WC1B 3DP, UK
1385 Broadway, New York, NY 10018, USA
29 Earlsfort Terrace, Dublin 2, Ireland

BLOOMSBURY, METHUEN DRAMA and the Methuen
Drama logo are trademarks of Bloomsbury Publishing Plc

First published in Great Britain 2022

A catalogue record for this book is available from the British Library.

A catalog record for this book is available from the Library of Congress.

ISBN: PB: 978-1-3503-8170-4
ePDF: 978-1-3503-8172-8
eBook: 978-1-3503-8171-1

Series: Modern Plays

Typeset by Mark Heslington Ltd, Scarborough, North Yorkshire
Printed and bound in Great Britain

Writer/Performer	**Anoushka Lucas**
Developed with and Directed by	Jess Edwards
Script Consultant	Tia Bannon
Dramaturgy	Daniel Bailey and Deirdre O'Halloran
Production and Company Stage Manager	Ruth Burgon
Set & Costume Designer	Georgia Wilmot
Lighting Designer	Laura Howard
Sound Designer	Bella Kear

Writer/Performer – Anoushka Lucas

Anoushka is a writer, singer, songwriter, composer and actress. Her music has been championed on Radio 2, where she has appeared on the Jamie Cullum show and BBC Introducing, and she was the inaugural winner of Jazz FM's Love Supreme Competition in 2013. She has sold out shows at the Cheltenham Jazz Festival, the 606 and Bush Hall to name a few, and has supported Tom Odell, Sophie Ellis-Bextor and Ashley Henry. Her debut album *Dark Soul* was released in 2019.

As a theatre composer, Anoushka co-composed an original score for *Klook's Last Stand* (Park Theatre, 2014/NAMT Festival 2017) with Omar Lyefook, and *The Etienne Sisters* (Theatre Royal Stratford East, 2015) with Sheila Atim and Nikki Yeoh – both with books by Che Walker. Anoushka also composed and performed in *Sparks* (Radio 4) by Jessica Butcher.

As an actor, Anoushka played Mary Magdalene in the Olivier Award winning *Jesus Christ Superstar* (Regent's Park Open Air Theatre, 2016), Katherine of France in *Henry V* (Donmar, 2022) and Laurey Williams in *Oklahoma* (Young Vic, 2022), among others, and must stay different.

Developed with and Directed by Jess Edwards

Jess Edwards is a Queer writer and director who splits her time between Margate and Tottenham in North London. Directing credits include: *Funeral Flowers* (Roundhouse and UK tour); *Albatross* (Playground Theatre); *Hotter/Fitter* (Soho Theatre); *Sparks* (HighTide / Radio 4 / Pleasance); *The Other Tchaikovsky* (Radio 4); *Passengers* (Summerhall / Adelaide Fringe); *Nacktsängerin* (BKA-Theater, Berlin); *Denim: World Tour* (Soho Theatre / Underbelly); *Punts* (Theatre503); *Torch* (New Diorama / Underbelly); *The Itinerant Music Hall* (Lyric Hammersmith / Latitude); *The Box* (Theatre Deli / Latitude); *Jekyll & Hyde* (Southwark Playhouse / Assembly).

Jess has worked as an associate director at the the Young Vic, Almeida, Theatre Royal Bath and in the West End. She has won the Summerhall Lustrum Award for *Passengers* and the Best New Musical Award for *Sparks*. In 2021 she was awarded a Developing Your Creative Practice grant from the Arts Council for her writing. She is currently workshopping her first play, creating a new musical with Trafalgar Entertainment Group, and developing two original screenplays.

Script Consultant – Tia Bannon

Tia Bannon is an actor, photographer, writer and artist.

She trained at RADA.

As an actor, she was nominated for Best Actress in a Play at the BBTA's 2021 for her performance as Kara in seven methods of killing kylie jenner at the Royal Court Theatre, Downstairs. She recently played Electra in *Oresteia* at the Park Avenue Armory, NYC.

As a writer, in 2021 her work was long-listed for the Nan Shepherd Prize and she is a recipient of the London Writers Award 2022. She is currently working on her first book.

Dramaturgy – Daniel Bailey and Deirdre O'Halloran

Daniel Bailey is Associate Artistic Director of the Bush Theatre. He was previously Associate Director at Birmingham Repertory Theatre, originally joining The REP as part of the Regional Theatre Young Director Scheme and where his work included artist development programmes for writers, theatre-makers and directors.

He has previously been Resident Director at the National Theatre Studio, Associate Artist at Theatre Stratford Royal East and Resident Assistant Director at The Finborough Theatre. Daniel studied Modern Drama at Brunel

University before participating in the Young Vic's Introduction to Directing.

His previous theatre directing credits include: *Red Pitch* (Bush Theatre); *The High Table* (Bush Theatre); *Unknown Rivers* (Hampstead Theatre); *My Darling Wife* (Talawa Theatre Company); *Pre Judgment Day* and *Covered* (New Heritage Theatre). His film director credits include: *On Belonging* (Young Vic); *Malachi* (S.E.D); *Floating On Clouds* (Kingdom Entertainment Group) and *Y.O.L.O. Therapy* (S.E.D).

Deirdre O'Halloran is the Literary Manager at the Bush Theatre, working to identify and build relationships with new writers, commission new work and guide plays to the stage.

At the Bush she's dramaturged plays including Olivier Award winner *Baby Reindeer* by Richard Gadd, *Lava* by Benedict Lombe and *An Adventure* by Vinay Patel.

Deirdre was previously Literary Associate at Soho Theatre, where she worked as a dramaturg on plays including *Girls* by Theresa Ikoko and *Fury* by Phoebe Eclair-Powell. She led on Soho Theatre's Writers' Lab programme and the biennial Verity Bargate Award.

As a freelancer, Deirdre has also been a reader for Out of Joint, Sonia Friedman Productions and Papatango.

Production and Company Stage Manager – Ruth Burgon

Ruth Burgon has worked across a wide range of theatre productions taking on many roles on both tours and in-house productions, specialising in new writing and the different opportunities that offers. More recently, Ruth has worked in production management with eStage and enjoyed the many possibilities this has presented, including being the Production Manager for the premier Bush Studio Season.

Credits in stage management include: *Games for Lovers* (The Vaults); *Coming Clean* (Trafalgar Studio); *Here* (Greenwich Theatre); *Broken Glass*, *Elton John's Glasses* and *Aladdin* (Watford Palace Theatre).

Credits in production management include: *Never, Not Once* (Park90); *Anthem, Horizon, We Are Here, Back Up!* (Bush Theatre, Community); *Invisible, Clutch, Elephant, Kola Nut Does Not Speak English* (Bush Theatre, Studio Season). Ruth is a graduate of LAMDA, where she studied Production and Technical Theatre, Stage and Screen, and Telford College, Edinburgh, where she studied Theatre Costume.

Set & Costume Designer – Georgia Wilmot

After graduating with a degree in Interior Design from Liverpool John Moores University Georgia worked on *Misfits* S3 (Channel 4); and as a costume trainee on *Monroe* (ITV) before deciding that set design was something to be explored.

Georgia's set and costume credits include: *Covered* (New Heritage Theatre at Paddington Arts Centre); Superdrug's YouTube channel Christmas campaign 2017, *I Knew You* (Birmingham Repertory Theatre); *Days of Significance* (Questors Theatre). In 2018 Georgia had the opportunity to create concept designs and illustrations for designer Tim McQuillen-Wright for Secret Cinema's *Blade Runner*. In 2021 Georgia designed sets for the Bush Theatre, Project 2036; *Pawn* (by Devon Muller); *One Day* (by QianEr Jin) and *LimBo* (by Latekid). In August 2021 Georgia returned to the Bush to design the set and costume for the Young Company introductory performance *Back Up!* (devised and directed by Katie Greenall).

Lighting Designer – Laura Howard

Laura is a Lighting and Sound Designer originally from Croydon. They graduated in 2020 from LAMDA's

Production and Technical Arts course and was a recipient of the William and Katherine Longman Charitable Trust Scholarship.

Assistant Lighting Designer credits include: *Amadigi* (English Touring Opera) and *Constellations* (Donmar/West End).

Lighting Designer credits include: *Elephant*, *The Kola Nut Does Not Speak English*, *Clutch* and *Invisible* (Bush Theatre); *Manorism* (Southbank Centre); *Exodus* (National Theatre Scotland); *Juniper and Jules*, *Splintered* and *curious* (Soho Theatre); *Dead Air* (Stockroom); *Moreno* (Theatre 503); *Cell Outs* (Camden People's Theatre); *We Never Get Off At Sloane Square* (Drayton Arms); *SHUGA FIXX vs The Illuminati* (Relish Theatre); *The Moors*, *Three Sisters*, *I Hate it Here*, *Sparks*, *Nine Night*, *The Laramie Project* (LAMDA).

Sound Designer – Bella Kear

Bella graduated LAMDA in July 2021 with a First-Class Honours Degree in Production and Technical Arts, specialising in sound. Credits as a Sound Designer include: *Invisible*, *Clutch* and *Elephant* (Bush Theatre); *Whose Planet Are You On?* (The Old Vic); *The Animal Kingdom* (Hampstead Theatre); *The Night Woman* (The Other Palace); *First Love is the Revolution* (E15); *The Faith Machine* (RADA); *Pelican Daughters* and *Education, Education, Education* (ArtsEd); *Darling* (The Hope Theatre); *Flux* (Theatre503).

Credits as an Associate Sound Designer include: *Seven Methods of Killing Kylie Jenner* (Swedish Transfer); *Purple Snowflakes* (Royal Court); *Blue/Orange* (Theatre Royal Bath); *A Place For We* (Talawa, The Park).

Acknowledgements

This play would not exist in this form without the expert guidance of Jess Edwards – my director, dramaturg and friend. Thank you, thank you, thank you. With deep thanks also to all at the Bush Theatre, especially Lynette, Daniel and Dee, who convinced me that I could and should write a play. Who knew? (You knew.)

Magic mentions to my readers along the way: Jess Butcher, Tia Bannon and my excessively literary sisters Natalia and Louella (harsh AND loving; dream combo). Thanks also to my agents at Curtis Brown for their constant support in every form.

Last, but not least, thanks to Mum and Dad, who got me a piano when I was seven, and never once doubted that I would grow up and make a living writing songs. You are crazy and I love you.

Elephant

This show must be performed by a piano player.

Where possible, this show should be performed with a real acoustic piano.

Original music should be written for any production of this show. There are lyrics to open and close the show, to be set to music. After that, where there is a stage direction 'Song' it's up to you – either an instrumental piece or a song with lyrics can be composed.

Anything spaced on the right is a Voice Over from outside. Each Voice Over is a different kind of voice (RP/MLE/regional) representing a variety of record label execs.

Rules on speech marks: if a character speaks without speech marks, their voice/accent can blend with Lylah's. If a character's text is in speech marks, it is resolutely different to Lylah's voice and must stay different.

88 Keys

There are 88 keys on a piano.
52 of the keys are white
36 of the keys are black.
The white keys are called tones
And the black keys are called semi-tones

Which means half tone
So the black keys are like
Half of a white key.

You take your finger
The fleshy pulpy part at the very end
And you curve your hand
As though something
Precious
Is right under your palm
And no matter what your fingers do
Or your wrists
Or your arms
You mustn't let your palm fall or you will squish
The precious thing

You take your finger
And you press a key
And inside the piano
There is a row
Of 88 hammers
Tiny little hammers
Wrapped in felt
Or leather
And when you press the key

It acts as a sort of lever
The hammer is released and hits against
A string
And the string
Vibrates
Which makes

Sound.

She starts to play the piano. Sparse at first, and then it builds.

The sound rolls around inside
The sound sneaks into all the spaces it can find
All the corners and edges and gaps
And it fills them so completely that it pours out
Out out
Into the room

The vibrations of the sound
Cause the air particles around the piano to vibrate
And those particles vibrating
Causes the air particles around them
To vibrate as well
So that pretty soon
All of the air particles in the room
Are vibrating
responding
To the piano

The room is vibrating

And as the particles
Influence the particles
They reach your ear
And your ear
recognises the vibration
And in response
Your ear drum
begins
To vibrate.

So when I hit the key
And the tiny felt hammer
Hits the string
And the string starts to vibrate

The sound
Inside the piano
Travels
Into you

And we are all
Vibrating
Together.

And then we can begin.

A moment of silence.

Then:

> (*Sung.*) Oceans and rivers and deep dark
> earth under the green
> Tell me the story of everywhere you've ever been
> Sing me the waves under your scars
> Show me the pieces of your heart
> Show me
> Show me
> Show me
> Show me

Piano Arrives (1996)

The piano is arriving today. I am 7.

A tall thin man and a short fat man come to deliver it in a lorry.

There are 4 of us in the flat:

Mum and Dad sleep in the living room
Sister and I sleep in the bedroom
Woodchip walls
Bunk bed
Glow in the dark stars on the ceiling.

Our flat is a council flat.

When you tell people you live in a council flat, they think you mean you live on an estate, but council flat just means 'a flat the council owns'.

In our case, the council owns a row of pretty little Victorian houses behind the hospital.

The men with the piano look up at our little flat

The narrow, narrow staircase,
The wobbly bannister
The sloping roof at the top of the stairs,
And they turn to Dad, light their fags, and say

'We might have to take the windows out'

Dad nods
Gravely
And the three men stand on the pavement and stare up at our flat.

Then they take the windows

The actual windows

Out of the wall.

Suddenly there is all this sky – light and blue and warm – pouring in onto the red afghan rug

And through the sky
Swinging like some kind of
Pirate ship
Comes this huge
Creaking
Warm
Brown
Beast

We rearrange the whole living room to fit the piano
The TV into the corner
The green chest of drawers goes back against the wall
Everything in our house is pink, or orange, or red, or blue, or green
Dad likes colours
He says it's important to see
How bright life can be

Dad says his Mum taught him that.

Dad's mum died when he was 8
She was from India
And she was what they used to call high yellow
And very beautiful.

I look a lot like his mum
Dad covers my face with his hand like this to show me
Look Lylah
He says
the bottom of your face is more your mother's
But this part
This part is my mother's.

My mouth is a bit more like Mum's dad.
Mum's dad was from Cameroon
And he came to France to play football
And he married my granny who was porcelain white and I
think for a while they were very happy
Except people spat at them all the time
And called him names
So he decided to go home.
He left when Mum was 5.

I asked Dad once
What's India like?

And he said

I don't know.

I asked Mum
What's Cameroon like?

And she said

I don't know.

Everything in our flat looks different now. With the piano
here.

Mum says

Tu ne joues pas après 8 heures
Tu ne joues pas Dimanche matin
Tu ne joues pas avant tes devoirs

I stand with Dad
The smoke from his jazz cigarette curls up into the ceiling
Mum is wiping down the piano
Bit of Pledge
Bit of cloth

She looks at me.

Bon, she says
Vas-y
Vas-y.

Meet and Greet (2015)

Urgh We're so excited to be meeting you like
Properly Excited
Lotta buzz around you
Lotta buzz Lotta buzz

So I guess this chat
It's informal really
I think we're just wondering like
How do you
See
You
You know?

Pocket (2017)

There are 6 record labels circling me and they say they want
to sign my album. I am doing lots and lots of gigs.

Today I am in a rehearsal room
In East London
waiting for my band

I am extra nervous because my usual drummer isn't here

He's sending his mate to replace him
His mate is late.

Suddenly the door swings open

This man walks in

He says
Sorry Jesus Fuck I'm so sorry I'm so sorry
I couldn't find any parking

Blue Jeans
Denim shirt
Open a bit too far down
Obviously he has an earring

He says
the traffic was a nightmare and then the parking on top –
I'm not normally late
I'm so sorry

He runs his hands through his curly blonde hair
puts his cymbal bag down
strides over to me

You must be Lylah
He says

He grins

I say
Hi
You must be
Leo

He says
Listen let me set up I'll just slot in with you guys

I say
Well we can talk you through the set –

He says
Nah nah it's fine it's fine
I listened on my way over
You just play
I'll catch up

I sing the opening verse
And I try to stay in the song
But I am distracted by his cymbal tightening
And the sticks coming out
And his jacket coming off
And his phone flashing up on the kick drum

This man takes up a lot of space

Music in.

He hits the shit rehearsal snare with a growl

He starts to play
Gentle
But strong
He sits right back in the pocket

He's
really fucking good

Music in. A sparse, sexy, steady beat.

I've never heard the drums sound like this before
Like a musical instrument
Like there are tones and colours in the skins

I shout
This is the middle 8

He nods

I say just follow me

We're going to push the 2 and the 4?
he nods
He does it

And then inexplicably slots a fill into the end of the line that
I swear has no space there

his sleeves are rolled up over his forearms
his hair's falling over one eye
He looks straight at me
His eyes are
grey

He shouts over the music

Lylah!
Go back to the top of that!

Top of what?

He says
'Harder than I've ever known'

Music out.

No drummer in the history of drummers has ever quoted
lyrics back to me
Drummers do not listen to lyrics

He says
Drop an A on the top of that chord

Music back in.

It is like the other two boys have disappeared

A?

Yeah yeah yeah

I push the A

Like this?

It sounds

She pulls a face. It is a good face.

He grins at me.
It is a good grin.

He says now push the 1!

And the 2!

And the 3!

Song.

Mahogany

My piano at home home is made from mahogany wood.

Mahogany wood grows in forests
In the Caribbean
And in Central and South
America.

There is a theory that the word mahogany
Comes from the Yoruba word
Oganwo

The men who cut the mahogany down
Were brought across oceans
They were enslaved
And they recognised the similarity
Of the tree growing in Jamaica
To the Khaya trees of West Africa.

Oganwo.

You can make beautiful things with mahogany.
Bed frames wall clocks tables chamber organs bookcases
chairs.

The earliest record of a mahogany object in the United
Kingdom is 1680. A cabinet.

When you cut down mahogany trees
You make a lot of new land
That should have trees
but doesn't

When they cut down all the mahogany trees
They made
Plantations
So this piano in *Europe*
left a hole
On *Caribbean* soil
That was covered up by
African hands.

I think about that a lot.

School (1996)

I am the only girl who looks like me in my class.

In fact now that I think about it I might be the only girl who looks like me in my year.

In fact now that I think about it, I think I might be the only girl who looks like me in my school.

I am on an enormous bursary from the French government to go here.
Mum just has to fill in a form every year to say how poor we are
and the government reads the forms and then they pay for me to go here
Because I am a French citizen.

The better my grades are, Mum says, the more money we get so it's important that I do my best to be the best every day.

Everyone at school is always saying what a beautiful mother I have
How exotic she is.

All the other mums kind of look like
Princess Diana

But my mum is all bright pink dreadlocks, box fresh
Reeboks, deep brown skin, denim mini skirts
And I think –
Well she is definitely the coolest mum.

There is a lady in the canteen called Dawn
She looks like my mum
Deep deep brown
She always gives me extra big helpings
And pulls me into these big huge hugs
And tells me she is proud that I am here

Hugging Dawn is so nice because her breasts smell like
lemons
But
It's also a bit embarrassing
No one else hugs canteen ladies
So lately I have started hiding in the toilets when I see her
around.

All the teachers like me a lot
I am
Good at reading
Good at writing
And I never ever get into trouble

I really like being good at school

I don't know why people find it so hard.
You just have to learn all of the rules
And then you follow them
And then everyone says you are special and good.

One of the rules at school is you have to speak French in the
classroom
But if you want to be cool you have to speak English in the
playground.
I make friends with all the other girls who like to speak
English like me.

It's funny cos different words mean different things in
English and French

Like for example
Blue in English is spelled
B-L-U-E
And it means a colour
But it also means
A feeling
And bleu in French is spelt
B-L-E-U
And it means a colour
But it also means
A bruise
Because in French a bruise is always blue
I don't know what colour a bruise is in English.

Sometimes we play this game where all the English speaking
girls stand at one end of the playground
And all the French speaking girls stand at the other one
And we run across saying mean things to each other. It's
really fun.

Iris says that Apolline's house is in a dustbin
And then Elodie says that Zoscia only eats custard and poo at
home nothing else
I am trying to think of something super good and horrible
And then Sarah runs over and says that Apolline said that
my family doesn't have a bathroom
And I am covered in years and years of dirt
Because I have never taken a bath
And that is the reason I smell so bad
And the reason why my skin is brown

Then after lunch I get picked to play the piano for the
summer party in the park and Mum says I am doing very
well and she is proud of me.

Toasties (2017)

She plays. Something gentle and sexy and sweet.

The first time Leo and I kiss is late afternoon.

Leo has an entire studio set up in his room
He rents this huge room on a big wide street in Hoxton
And he only pays £400 a month because his mate owns it

He has all his kit in here
Leo has loads and loads of kit

He teaches on the side at this big music university

Leo went there
He did jazz
And he knows
The names
Of all the chords
I don't know the names of
In my own songs

Mum wouldn't let me do music
She said it wasn't a safe degree
I did languages instead

Leo plays me music
He plays me Bill Evans and Keith Jarrett and Steely Dan
and Oscar Peterson and Leonard Bernstein and Sergeant
Pepper (but on vinyl) and Donny Hathaway live at the
Troubadour and Lalah Hathaway and Laura Nyro and
Snarky Puppy which he says is really really where jazz is at
now and Daniel Caesar and PJ Morgan

I play him my favourite Fiona Apple songs and Carla Bruni
and Françoise Hardy
We agree, objectively, that Rufus Wainwright is the greatest
lyricist of our time

He listens to all my songs and suggests records to listen to
He plays bass alongside me

Leo plays bass and keys and drums and guitar
Everything

We play and we play and we play

At some point we realise we forgot to eat
so we walk to the coffee shop on the Green
And stand outside
Waiting for our toasties

It's a bit awkward
Away from the music

I say
God there are so many pushchairs round here
He says
Yeah I know it's like yummy mummy central
I say
Isn't that a weird expression yummy mummy, like it's an
anomaly to be a mother *and* attractive
And he laughs and says you're so right I've never thought of
that before
We're talking but we're not really listening to anything we're
saying
He's looking at me
Looking at me
And then

he kisses me

Very gently
For a long time

I kiss him back
No tongues or anything
Just
Simple

Song.

I've loved a few people before
But it's not usually like this

The thing inside me
Is the same
As the thing inside Leo

And when I make music
He can hear
All of me.

Music out.

Alicia Keys (2016)

Do you like Alicia Keys?

Yeah cos there's never been an English Alicia Keys has there
No one quite so
Sort of
Musically driven
I mean
That was something they pushed with her wasn't it
That was the angle
The piano
The songwriting

Unusual really

I think Alicia Keys is
The ideal
Choice of reference for you you know
Because you're clearly –

And I think to begin with
We'd probably want to start with more
Straightforward songs
You know?
More
Accessible.

And at the piano
Wow
Amazing

So hot to just have you
There
Together.

So can we have a think about more
Stripped back vocals
More sort of big ballad stuff?

You know just sort of one long vowel
Ooooooooh
I keep on falling
Iiiiiiiiiiiiiiiiiiiiiiin
Like that you know?

Really hit them with that noise.
No one wants
too many words
to begin with.

She plays the piano.

Let Them be Jealous (2017)

When Leo and I first sleep together
We basically stay in bed
For 2 days

He runs his fingers over my collarbone
And my neck
my breasts
my belly
And I trace the freckles on his shoulders

He tells me his grandma was Danish
And his grandad was English
And his dad went to boarding school
And worked in the city

I tell him
My mum's dad was from Cameroon
And my dad's mum was from India

And my mum's mum was from France
And my dad's dad was from Dorset

He says
What's Cameroon like

I say
I don't know

We open the curtains on the second day and never close
them again
We're on the first floor
And besides, Leo says
Who cares if people see
Let them be jealous

Outside some schoolchildren are fighting over a bag of chips

Song.

After 3 days at Leo's house I want to go home
I refuse to keep wearing Uniqlo boxer shorts when we go
outside
And I also cannot use his 2in1 Head and Shoulders
Shampoo
So my hair is getting all
Matted
And the frizz Halo is
Out of control.

Leo says stay
He pulls me into him
What are you talking about
He says
You look beautiful like this
Earthy
Wild woman.
I love it.

Piano out.

Brown princess.

Mum (1996)

Mum says it's really important to just
Rise above
stupid things that people say.

I told her about Apolline saying my skin is brown because I
don't take baths
And she said
Non mais les gens racontent toujours n'importe quoi Lylah
Just ignore them.

Dad shouts from the kitchen that Apolline is probably just
repeating what her parents say
Cos her parents are Swiss aristocrats
Everybody knows Swiss aristocrats are actually Nazis!
Mum says
Mais n'importe quoi!
You know full well Switzerland was neutral in the war
Dad shouts back
There is No Such Thing as a Neutral Aristocrat!
And then Mum says that we should also ignore Dad.

Mum is brushing my hair.

Mum brushes my hair and brushes my hair and brushes my
hair every evening.

Sois sage Lylah, she says
Sois sage
Which means
Behave Lylah
Behave

Well actually it means
Be wise Lylah
But be wise means be-have in French so –

Mum tells me
I am so lucky
To have such beautiful hair
So lush

And long
And good.

See how it goes down down down
Not like her silly hair which goes up up up.

Mum changes her hair all the time
It used to be relaxed
And then it was in braids
And then it was cropped
And dyed bleach blonde.

I asked Mum if I can have mine
Short like hers
But she said no no
You should keep your hair long
To show how beautiful it is
How special
And good.

When Mum was little
She lived with some nuns in France
And they told her and Tata Mathilde that their hair
Was a punishment from God
That if their mother had been pure
Their hair would have been prettier

Mum says
The nuns were stupid
And evil
But she does also say
That my hair is
better.

I like it when Mum brushes my hair
It sort of hurts but it's nice when Mum and I just
chat.

It is the only time Mum and I have together.

She is working all the time now
Doing teacher training

teaching adult education French
And Dad is working lots too
Climbing up and down ladders
Painting skirting boards and ceilings.

Mum and Dad are working and working and working so
that we can save enough money to
Buy the flat.

At the beginning when they said they were buying the flat,
Dad got very angry and said it was a social aberration and he
wasn't doing it because it was bloody Margaret Thatcher's
idea
But Mum got very angry then and said it's not bloody
Margaret Thatcher's idea, it's my idea!
And then they argued a lot and now we are buying the flat.

Mum says that when we buy the flat we can build a second
bedroom in the loft
And Sister and I can have a big bedroom up under the sky
And Mum and Dad can have our room now and stop
sleeping in the living room
So the living room will be only for
Eating and
Watching TV
And playing the piano.

Music in.

Une grande chambre sous les étoiles Lylah.

I try to imagine
A room inside the ceiling
But it's hard to imagine something that doesn't exist.

You know?

Song.

Cousins (still 1996)

Every other Sunday we go and visit my cousins on the other
side of the river.

My cousins live in a council flat that IS on an estate.

Every time we see my cousins they have a different hairstyle.

Today we walk in and they have a hundred round bobbles
each, every colour
Red
Purple
Blue
Pink
Splitting their hair into a hundred different sections.

I am so jealous.

We play school again
We always play school
I always have to be the teacher
Because I am weird and boring
And I talk white like a teacher.

Uncle Errol tells my cousins to ease up now
I love Uncle Errol
Uncle Errol is married to Tata Mathilde
Mum's sister.
He goes home to Jamaica a lot
But now he is back
And that means

Curry goat for dinner.

When you eat curry goat, Uncle Errol says, you can't say
'Thank you very much for the nice goat curry'
You have to say 'that's a mean curry goat'
Uncle Errol says 'Thass a meeeaaann curry goat Uncle
Errol' like that and when I say it back he laughs and laughs
and laughs and calls out to my dad 'That school turning
your daughter into the Queen' but before I can get upset he

drops down to my face and says
'Now then
I'm only teasing
How you talk is your own business'
And you should be might proud
To sound like a proper English lady

My big cousin shows me how to suck the meat off the bone
I love it

I asked Mum why we don't have curry goat at home and she
said quiche is much easier.

My cousins and Sister and I count up all the bone bits on our
plates
In the living room all the grown ups are smoking jazz
cigarettes and listening to Lauryn Hill.

Sometimes we stay over at my cousins
I don't like that very much.
Uncle Errol's jazz cigarettes smell different to Dad's
And nobody speaks French here
My cousins speak Patois
They say they know they are from Cameroon
But their real culture is Pure Island

I don't know what Pure Island means

When we stay over
Tata Mathilde
Puts all these pommades in my hair
That make it go
Flat flat.

Tata Mathilde looks a lot like Mum
Dad says they are both very beautiful
They look like their father
Cheekbones!

Mum and Tata Mathilde don't remember their dad cos he
left when they were so little
But they have photos

Mum hates looking at the photos
But Tata Mathilde has them on the wall.

When she does my hair, Tata Mathilde says Mum should be
putting these pommades on me every day
'Comme tes cousines'

I don't know how to tell Tata Mathilde
that I can't have flat flat hair at school
Nobody at my school has flat flat hair
They just have nice hair
So if I stick mine down
I will not
Fit in.

I don't have to tell Mum this because she just understands.

Speaking Voice (2017)

And about the way you speak

Have you always spoken like that?

It's lovely
lovely
Your parents must be so
Proud

It's just not very –
It doesn't make you very
Approachable

I wonder if you could just try
Rounding it off a bit
Making it a bit more
Accessible
A bit more sort of

Proper London London

You know?

Cos I think we want to pitch the sort of
Council flat beginning you know
And
you've got such a soulful tone
So sort of
I mean that kind of voice tells a story doesn't it?
Pain
Struggle
And we want to make sure it's a story your speaking voice
Tells as well.

Hmm?

Ivory

At a certain point – a bit later than now but the idea can begin now – blood should start to seep out from under the piano.

The keys of a piano
For a long time they were made out of
Ivory

From elephant tusk.

People think an elephant tusk means the thing that
protrudes from an elephant's face
But that is only
two-thirds
Of an elephant tusk.

The first third of the tusk

The root

Is embedded deep inside the elephant's skull
Under the eyes

Around the tusk there is a
Soft wet cavity
Pulpy and warm
And within that cavity

There are thousands and thousands
Of nerves
And tissue
And blood vessels

The tusk
The strongest part of the tusk
Is nestled into this cavity
So
The toughest part of an elephant
Is inside
The softest part.

You can't just
Remove a tusk
That would be cruel
And unspeakably painful

It's better
Much better
To just

Kill the elephant

She plays the piano. It takes us back to Leo. Underscore stays in.

Growing (2017)

Leo and I move in together.
It's really nice.

We've started playing this game where we write songs
together
Cos I told him when I met him
I can't write songs when anyone else in the room.

When I told him that he looked at me like I was *insane* and
he said
What do you mean?!

And I said
I was sort of embarrassed about it
But I said
I'm serious
I have to be on my own in a room
With the door shut
And no noise of anyone else
I have to forget anyone else exists

It's always been like that

I tell him how when I was a kid I used to practise my piano
And when I was really little Mum would help me do my
scales and things
Even though she never knew what they were
But then as I got older
I'd just go and do it on my own
For half an hour
And it was like magic
Because as soon as I started playing
I had a whole room
To myself

I tell him that's how the first songs happened
I was limping through some Handel
Bored and probably murdering it
And then nobody was there
Monitoring me
Checking I was doing the right thing
So I pushed my whole hand down
Down down
I don't remember thinking I was going to write a song
I just started playing loads of keys together to see what they
sounded like
Not the chords I'd been taught just noises
together
And then I'd play some other noises together and loop
round and round

And then words just started
Coming out

Leo laughs and laughs and says
Lylah
That's great but collaboration is the foundation of music
You can't still need to do it on your own!

I feel funny
I hate when he does this laughing at me joke thing

I say
Yeah but
Sometimes when you play with other people they sort of
Take over

He says
Take over?
No one's taking over – it's music! We all share it!

I say
Yeah but sometimes when I –

When you what?

I don't know just sometimes when I sort of
When someone else gets involved
I lose sight of like
What I was trying to say.

Leo says
I think the best idea always wins out anyway. You know?

I say
Yeah.

I guess.

Yeah.

Song.

Pianos (2001)

Everyone at school has a piano
And everyone does
Piano lessons.

When I go for sleepovers at my friends' houses
I always leave and go and find the piano
Which all my friends say is weird and lame.

Iris's piano is in her family parlour.
I learned the word parlour when I went to Iris's house
And I also learned the word pantry
And townhouse.

Zoscia's piano is in her second living room
Nobody calls Zosica's second living room the parlour
because her family is Polish
It's the room where the TV is set to French
And there are always lots of newspapers on the table
Because her dad is
A politician

The words for living room in English are
Living room lounge parlour front room sitting room
Someone at school has a drawing room
but I don't know how that's different
I haven't seen it
In French it's salon
in Italian it's
Soggiorno
which I really like
Because soggiorno sounds like sojourn
I'm learning Italian at school now
Sojourn is a holiday in English
Anyway then there is a word for open plan kitchen
Which is sort of like a living room
Or salon salle à manger
So that's when the room has
Two functions

Nobody has a word though for when your living room
Is also an eating room
And a bedroom
In any language.

Which is sort of odd when you think about it because
There are so many words.

Musical (2014)

Now the other thing we're a bit concerned about is
You know
It sort of seems like some of your songs are quite
Theatrical!
And that's

I mean we want to avoid that
I mean, looking at this list you've given us

You know
Fiona Apple...
Regina Spector...
Martha Wainwright...
I mean, great artists but
Is that the right sort of sound
For *you*

You know
We think you've got way more
Soul
Than those people
And we'd hate to
Lose that
So early.

Building (1998)

There are builders everywhere in the flat.

There is a plastic sheet where the kitchen doorway should be
And where the telephone was in the corner
Now there is a ladder
A big tall metal ladder with flecks of paint on every step and
men in boots climbing up and down it all day long
Shouting 'Incoming!'
Or
'Who wants what?'

All the men in boots know my dad and they like him a lot.
Their boss is called Frank.

Mum and Dad are really tired all the time now.

Dad is working Saturday and Sundays
And Mum is teaching full time
And when Sister and me do homework, Mum does
homework too.
She says we are a homework club!

Mum shouts a lot during homework club.

Then when the builders leave I'm allowed to play.

Mum sits and listens.

She plays.

C'est magnifique Lylah
Dad comes in.
Sister stays in the bedroom.
There's no more noise anymore.

I like it when everybody listens.

Genius (2018)

The blood is definitely trickling out from under the piano now.

Leo is really busy. He is being offered session after session
after session

He's working all the time and he is exhausted and we never
fucking see each other anymore

I'm stressed

Two more labels have turned me down this week
I don't know what to do with my songs
I am doing them wrong
Nobody wants them.

Leo keeps playing with all these amazing people
Lianne La Havas
Laura Mvula
Mahalia
He says he's probably going to spend a lot of this summer on
tour
I can go with him.

It's cool he's got so much work.

It's sort of funny there's like a little gang of them
Boys he went to uni with
And they're all in on these sessions
This little indie-jazz gang
Depping on all the same gigs.

We went to a party the other week
Everyone kept saying
'Oh so you're Lylah! Heard so much about you!'
And then 3 people said: 'Oh My God, Leo's a genius, isn't
he?'
And I said
'Yeah. He's really special.'

Some cool label people were there
All men obviously.
And all the sessions guys.
And the in house sound engineer.

They all looked –

Well Leo and the sound engineer had the same hat.

She is trying to articulate the fact that the room was entirely white
men, but she cannot say that sort of thing out loud.
She plays the piano then stops.

Tusk Transport

Once you've killed the elephant
You have to cut open its face
To extract the tusk.

You can do this pretty quickly once the elephant is dead

In the 1500s
Before the Transatlantic trade began
It is estimated that there were
25 million elephants
On African soil
Now today
There are
416,000
So that's
A lot of dead elephants.

After a gentleman on safari had shot the elephant
He'd have his picture taken with the corpse
And then he'd go to dinner
And someone else would
Remove the tusk.

Then to sell the tusk
You have to transport them
To market
On the coast.

Carrying a tusk is really difficult because they are very heavy.
The average tusk weighs about 20 kg
And takes up to 4 men to carry.

The easiest thing before was just to tie 4 enslaved people
together

One by one in a row
And then place the tusk over their shoulders
And then they could carry the tusk
From deep inside the mainland
To the coast
For you.

Lineage (2018)

Leo says
Because I'm a bit down
We should go and stay at his parents' house
It's really beautiful down there
Deep countryside
And besides
He says
They're sort of annoyed they haven't met you.

Leo's parents' house is

Big.

He called it a cottage in London
And his mum called it a cottage in the car
And I know his grandmother lives there as well
But I am surprised to discover that the cottage
Has
9 bedrooms
And a second house on the side
For guests?

We walk into the house
Leo's hand in the small of my back
the ceilings are very low

His dad comes out
Pink apron on
'Hullo hullo hullo
Here you are at last the floozy who stole my son's heart!'

Leo says
Dad!

I say
Ha

His dad says
'Leo tells me you're an Oxonian like myself! Which college
which college?'
And I say
Wadham

And he says
Oh god not a bloody socialist in the house!

I hear my voice changing as we walk through the door
I say Modern Languages
I say what a beautiful home you have
I say oh gosh that's lovely I'd love some tea yes please

Urban (2015)

Now the other option
And this is very popular
Very very popular
Especially when we're launching new female artists is
How would you feel about guest tracking
On a more sort of
Urban artist's track?

That can be very very helpful
Get you out there
Everyone sees you
Everyone hears your tone
And I think with your
look
We could team you up so easily with like
Tinie Tempah
Or
Stormzy

Have you heard of him?
Could be really good
You know

Push your authentic roots

Kenya (2018)

At dinner
Leo's grandmother asks me
When I started
Writing songs

His mum says
Gosh you're so talented!
Not like silly old us!
You're just made of magic aren't you!

There is a map on the wall
Hand drawn

I say
What's that?

Leo's dad says
Oh that –

Leo's mum says
Lylah you MUST have more potatoes

She stands up to dole them onto my plate

That was family land
He says
Where I grew up in Kenya

Leo's mum says
Where are your parents from Lylah?
I say
Oh well
Mum's half Cameroonian –

Leo says
Well you're English aren't you Ly, you're not Cameroonian

Leo's dad says
'West Africa! Glorious country!'

Leo's mum says
Gosh that'll be why you're so pretty
so exotic!

Leo's grandmother says
So your grandfather was –

I say
Cameroonian yeah
I turn to his dad
'So you grew up in –'

I don't know now if I should say Keeeenya or Kenya

Leo's dad says
Yes
Well
I came here for school
Obviously
But the farm was
Home
True home

He looks at the map

That dust road
My brother used to chase me down it for hours
I can still hear Father calling us in

I look at the map of the Kenyan farm on the wall

God it broke Father's heart
He says
Losing that farm
It was our home
Our farm
Our land

And they just
took it away

Leo says
Yeah Dad I think that's quite enough of a trip down
colonisers' memory lane

And his dad says
Oh for God's sake Leo not everything has to be so politically
correct I'm talking about my childhood. My father.

And his mum says
BOYS

And his grandmother says
Oh so you're a Quadroon!

I say
Wow, this gravy is really delicious. Thank you.

Upstairs (1998)

One Friday after school
It is raining
And Frank says to Dad
Right, want to come up?

Dad turns to me and says
What do you think, want to come up?

We climb the ladder.
Dad climbs behind me
I feel him behind my ankles
And as we climb he says
Well done Ly
Almost there

Even though we are inside our house
It is scary this ladder
Because this ladder is going

Through a hole in the ceiling
And I've never been inside the ceiling before

Suddenly I am through the hole
And there is light everywhere

In front of me there are 3 windows
The rain drums down onto them

I can see so far

Mum decides she will come up too
And then Sister says she wants to come
And I say
You're too small to come up
And Mum says
Lylah don't talk to your sister like that

We all stand inside the roof

Mum shows us where we will put the beds

When we put the beds up here
then I'll have my own bed
Like everyone at school
Not a bunk bed anymore

And my piano will be
In the living room
Like how everyone's piano is just
In the living room

And everything will be
The same
For us
As it is
For everyone else.

She tries to play but the weird sounds disturb her playing. Also she's got a bit of blood on her now and it's sticky and distracting.

After Dinner (2018)

At Leo's parents' house
After dinner
We 'retire to the drawing room'.

In the drawing room there is a huge fireplace and across the
ceiling there are two beautiful wooden beams.

Leo's mum tells me

'Oh those beams are ship beams
Centuries old!
They're repurposed isn't that clever
I just love knowing the house is secure
because they've lasted for years and years
Crossing oceans and seas
Carrying all sorts of cargo across the word
And now here they are
In my ceiling!
Isn't that something?'

At the far end of the drawing room is a deep mahogany baby
grand piano.

Leo pulls out some old sheet music
Starts playing some Chopin
Impromptu 89

I've never heard him play classical stuff before.

The fire glows

I'm a bit drunk.

When he is finished I say
That's a beautiful piano
Sounds so warm

And his father is delighted and says
'Isn't it!
Inherited it from my aunt

It's German
1930s'

I say isn't it amazing to think where that piano came from

And he says
'Quite quite
Been in my family for years'

I say
Is it ivory?

And his dad says
'Hmmm?'

I say
The keys
Are they ivory?

He says
'Well yes I expect so hahaha'

And I say
Did you know elephants have moon rituals?

And he says
'Is that so?'

Leo's mother interrupts
'Lylah now why don't you play us something? We'd love to
hear you sing! You must perform!'

I say
They think they do anyway.
They wrap their trunks around branches from trees
And they wave them
At the waxing moon
Actually also
there's anecdotal evidence
That they bathe
Every full moon

Leo's mum says
'Who does?'

I say
Elephants

I say
They have funerals as well.
They lay their trunks
On the bodies of their dead
Pick up their bones
Gently and in silence
And stand together

Leo's dad laughs and says
'Alright young lady. Enough filibustering. Time for a song
please!'

I say
Yeah and when an elephant dies
When the corpse is there
On the ground
And there's blood everywhere
And their tusk has been ripped out
Of the softest sweetest cavity
In their own face
I mean can you imagine that
Someone just ripping something out of your face?
Anyway after
If the herd finds them
Then they stay with them
For days
Just standing
All these elephants
Together
They cover it with leaves and grass
And soft things from the land
Like a ritual

Isn't that amazing?

They are all staring at me

I say
Don't you think that's amazing?

I say
I think about all that all the time.

Everytime I play the piano
I'm playing something ripped out of an animal's face
And transported by enslaved hands
across an ocean
And whittled down and carved
And now it's under my hand

And we all just
(I look at Leo's family)
Sorry
You
You all just go on pretending none of that ever happened
that this piano just miraculously appeared here in your
family
Out of nowhere
the result of European manufacturing genius
But like where did the materials come from?
You know?
Where does all this stuff you have now come from before?
You know?

Leo is looking at me across the room with a sort of
What the fuck are you doing face

I know
I say
I'm sorry
I know I'm not meant to talk about it it's rude

I'm being rude

I look at him

But what IS being rude?
Who decided the rules about what is rude and what is polite?

What are those rules for?
Because I know I'm supposed to sit here and be incredibly
charming about this gravy
And say thank you to your mum while she tells me she's got
Repurposed slave ship wood holding up her literal house
And your dad tells me he really misses his colonial land
But like
Come on guys.

There's so much British Empire in your living room.
In you.
It's here with us now.

And I feel like when I'm sat here
being called a Quadroon
And asked where I'm from
And told I am so lucky to be so exotic
And that my musical talent is a form of mystical magic
Not skill or work
I mean God forbid a brown woman could write music from
any place other than strange
instinctual magic
What you're actually doing
Is you're asking me to not react to racism
To confirm that it doesn't exist
And to show also that I am just like you
And how could a person like you
Have any connection
To that horrible history?
You didn't do any of that stuff.
It's all over!

And how could you be connected to it because
Good things can't possibly be connected to bad things.
That's too confusing.
That would be like a person being black AND white
or posh AND poor
or English AND European
No no no no no.

And the worst part is
I just keep going along with all of this
Because I want you to like me!
I'm in love with your son
And being just like you is lovely!
The dinners are so tasty and the conversation so pleasing

So I've learned to never really stop and think about
why my mum thinks long wavy hair
Is better
Than her own natural afro
Or why I've spent my entire life wishing I didn't have this
Frizz Halo around my head
Or how my dad said
People threw bricks through his window when he was a kid
Or how my mum doesn't know
Where she's from
Or how I wished my nose was more narrow when I was a kid
And I used to hold it pinched when I was falling asleep
Even though I had no understanding of why I wished that
It's just on some level thought I was ugly
Until one day I found out I could be exotic chocolate
caramel quadroon earth woman all the time
And then I learned I can be a very particular kind of
beautiful
Wild and earthy
And I learned to say yes
I do have an unnatural talent for jazz
Even though I'm not even sure
It's jazz that I make

Because I learned that everywhere
All of the time
People only ever want to see
a beautiful row of 88 ivory keys
That make up a piano

And no one wants to see
88 ivory keys

And also
A dead fucking elephant
24 million dead elephants killed over 5 centuries of
transatlantic trade
And a mahogany tree shipped over an ocean
After being cut down
By African hands

Nobody wants to think about that
It's frightening!
And sad
And nothing to do with us
But it's hard not to think about it
When it's who you are
So I've been expending a lot of energy really
hiding all the hard parts
For so long
And I'm tired
I'm really fucking tired
Of jump jump jumping between all these different versions
of me
That suit the room I am in
And of never complaining
About never being whole
So I'm just going to tell you now
When I look at the world
At our furniture
And our instruments
And the make up of our rooms
What I see is that everything is fucking connected to
everything
My history and your history are the same history
And I am still battling against it
And I'm doing all this work
hiding the parts of myself that do not fit right
And I'm only just realising that is expected of me
because it's in the interest
It has always been

in the interest
Of those in power
To make sure that people like me
Never connect
The parts to each other
To only show a part
And never be a whole
Because if I connect the parts
Everyone else will have to too.

Silence.

Lylah gives up.

A long ass John Cage Silence.

The Piano Speaks

I don't know what this is yet, but the piano has to save her.
They make something good
Together.

Connected

I promise I don't only think about murder when I play the
piano.
I think about everything when I play the piano
Even though it is the only time
I feel like
I am not really thinking at all.

I just am here.
With you.
My friend.

One elephant tusk
Can be used to make up
25 piano keyboards.

That means this piano here
Potentially
Has 24 other piano siblings
Dotted around
The city
Or the country
Or the continent.

You can't find those pianos though
Because nobody tracked what tusk became what objects.
That would have been a strange exercise.

They are connected though.
These objects in different rooms
Did come from
The same place
They've just been separated off.

My piano might think it's on its own
Because it lives here
in my mum and dad's living room
And it can't see other pianos that feel the same way.

But even if it feels that way.

It isn't on its own.

Nothing is on its own.

Record Label (2018)

So
Sorry
I think we've got a bit off topic here
How do you feel about
Those changes
Just ironing out the way you speak
Making the tracks more spacious
Dropping some of the lyrics
Collaborating with a more Urban artist

Is that something you'd be
Interested in?

Not really no.
Thank you.

Love (2018)

She plays the piano.

Leo and I ride home on the train in silence.

We left his parents early.

I feel bad.

You can't just go off on one like that Ly
Those are my parents.
You humiliated them.
You were a guest.

I say
Lee. I am so tired of feeling like a guest.

Leo says
What are you talking about?

I say
The possibility that I could get kicked out of the rooms I
move in
Has been in my mind
Since I was 4 years old.
And I am tired of it.

He says
I don't know what is going on. This is literally coming from
nowhere.

I say
I'm sorry
I'm not trying to be obtuse
I just
I can't keep pretending the differences between us don't
exist.

Leo says
What differences?
You make music, I make music. It's in your soul and in my
soul. We've always said that's all that
matters.

I say
It's not.

I say

When you walk into a music studio, all you have to think
about is the music. You never have to
police the way you talk, or the way you look, or the way you
behave in order to be accepted.
Nobody has ever thought any part of you is a contradiction
with another part of you. You are just
allowed to be your whole self.

Leo sighs.

He says

I don't understand what you want me to do.
I can't dismantle the world order for you Ly. I'm a session
player. Not Nelson Mandela.

I laugh.

I say
I know that.

He says.
I love you.

I say
I know that.

He says
I thought you loved me.

I look at him.
He looks really tired, and stressed, and his grey eyes are
staring deep into mine like I am the
only thing on planet earth.

I don't know what to say back to him.

I love him.
I love him so much he feels like home inside one person.
I don't want to break up with someone I love because we are different.
Difference should be surmountable.
But in his refusal to see the differences he makes me have to pretend.

He stares at me some more.

He says
Is this over?

I look at him.

I say
I don't know.

Adoption (2022)

It is 2022.

I am home. Home home. With the people who made me.

I sit at the piano.

I am on my own for a bit.
It's nice.

I've stopped trying to get a record deal.
I do not want to package myself up
It's a horrible exercise
I hadn't realised I'd been doing it for so long.

I was so busy trying to present a beautiful outside of me
I didn't take time to look at the hammers
And the strings
And the keys

And check I was okay.

Isn't it amazing what's inside the things in front of us? Isn't it amazing what we can see? We all of us, in this room, see different things in the spaces around us.

All those parts can be true at the same time.

She starts to play.

There are 88 keys on a piano.
And when you hit a key
A hammer is released
And it hits against
String
The string vibrates
Which makes
Sound
And the sound
Rolls around
And sneaks into every space it can find
Until it pours out
Out out
Into the room

And then

Everyone

Listens.

> (*Sung.*) Oceans and rivers and deep dark earth
> under the green
> Tell me the story of everywhere you've ever been
> Sing me the waves under your scars
> Show me the blood inside your heart
> I see
> I see
> I see

The End.